THE L

ANIMA

by
Naseem Ahsun

Illustrated by
Sarah Ray and Paris Ahsun Ransome-Williams

*Dear Jo
wishing you a
wonderful
adventure.
much love
N Ahsun
x*

About the Author

Naseem Ahsun, known as Naz, is an author, co-founder of Vision Maker Press, radio presenter on Swindon 105.5 and a consultant. She co-presents *The Outer Limits* with Paul Devlin and Simon Mundy and also presents The *Good News Show* with Ann Perrin.

Naz is passionate about stories and the power of stories to touch others deeply and bring people together.

She lives in Oxfordshire with her partner Laurence Gouldbourne, her children and her cat, Zeus.

To find out more about Naz, go to her website
www.naseemahsun.com
and her publishing website
www.visionmakerpress.com

THE LITTLE BOOK
OF
ANIMAL WISDOM

ISBN 978-1-9995849-0-0

First Published April 2018

Published by
Vision Maker Press

Printed in Great Britain

Contents

Dedication

For Laurence – my best friend, partner and so much more – with love always, Naz x

Acknowledgements

I would like to extend my deepest appreciation and gratitude to Laurence Gouldbourne: thank you for taking the time and care to edit this book, make Saturday soup for my soul and being your wonderful self – I love being with you.

To my amazing daughter, Paris Ahsun Ransome-Williams; thank you for your amazing chakra illustrations and your humour. You are such a gift.

To my wonderful son, Samuel Ahsun Ransome-Williams; thank you for your wisdom and honesty; I continue to learn so much from you and about you - you are an amazing man.

To my feline friend, Zeus; you are a gift to us all with your cuddles, purrs, playfulness and incredible gentleness. I love that you share my love of coffee!

To Sarah Ray of Design Marque; your generosity, kindness, humour and amazing ability as an artist are simply inspirational! I deeply value our friendship, connection and collaboration. This book would not be what it is, without you.

To Jennie Caswell; I will be forever grateful to you for inviting me to connect with the wisdom of the Power Animals. Without your guidance and invitation to step into the unknown, I would never have found the path that has led me to this book.

To Katie Speed; thank you for your encouragement and support. I am learning to trust myself more and more each day. I truly value our telephone conversations on days when I second guess my intuition and my gut.

To Rebecca Hanscombe and Zoe Mason; thank you for the healing and transformational experience of Ecstatic Awakening Dance. I truly value how you have taught me to surrender to my body. Through this amazing experience I have discovered the beauty of dancing with my Power Animals and, as a result, developed a deeper connection with them.

Finally, but not least, I am hugely grateful to my Power Animals who continue to offer me guidance, messages and invitations to widen my vision of the world and who I am. Thank you for leading me to all the places and people who have really supported me in being me and helped me to recognise that being me is enough, especially Ariel and Shya Kane and the Transformation Made Easy.

Wishing you all much love,

Naz x

Introduction

Our connection to the animal kingdom has been a continuous love affair. From the earliest history of humankind, we have been dependent on the animal kingdom and Nature for our very survival. When we consider the ancient civilizations of the Mesopotamians and Celts to the indigenous tribes of the worlds, such as the Salish, Apache and Lakota tribes of Northern America, Konkani people of South-Western India and Aborigines of Australia, it is clear that the interdependent relationship between humankind and Nature is an ancient one.

Irrespective of our high-speed, technology-filled world, our fascination, connection and love of animals continues to thrive. From cat and dog lovers; clothing brands such as Puma and Lacoste, to powerful car logos: Jaguar, Ferrari and Lamborghini. Even our very language is immersed with animal symbolism. e.g., *as angry as a hornet, as blind as a bat, eager beaver, as free as a bird.* When you begin gathering the evidence, it is astonishing really how much we still do maintain our connection with the animal kingdom.

So, is this just coincidence? Or is there something else at work? Something beyond the mechanical function of our minds?

In early 2012, my life was particularly stress-filled. High speed only touched the surface of how I was racing through my days, solely focused on my goals. It wasn't an existence I was particularly satisfied with, as I was essentially existing from one task to the next. No surprise really that my stress levels were high and my sense of wellbeing at an all-time low.

I recall a particular Sunday evening feeling especially down about my job, my home and my life in general. I felt lost, stuck in a quagmire, slowly sinking deeper and deeper into it. That's when I decided to call a close friend of mine and ask her advice on what I could do to get my life flowing again.

I don't quite know what I was expecting, but I certainly wasn't expecting the advice that she gave me – it felt like something out of *Avatar*! Her advice was to look for the answers through animal messengers, that she called Power Animals. If I slowed down, asked the Universe to send me a message through a Power Animal, then one would show up for me. I wondered how I would be able to tell the difference between a normal animal and Power Animal. My friend assured me that I would know, as the Power Animal would gain my attention by behaving in an unusual way. Feeling like I had nothing to lose, I decided to give it a go.

The next day, I felt more than a little foolish as I drove to work at half my usual speed, mentally asking the Universe to send me a message through a Power Animal. I wondered how the Universe was going to make this happen on a journey that mostly involved motorways? My scepticism seemed justified, as not one animal showed up - not even a gnat. By the time I drove into the car park, my disappointment was complete. I felt beyond stupid and even lower than the night before. How gullible was I? And, just as that thought crystalized, a miracle appeared.

As if by magic, a robin flew onto my side mirror and just sat there watching me. My heart hammered in my chest as I stared at the robin staring, intently, back at me. Its inquisitive black eyes communicated a self-assurance and calm that I had never felt before – a feeling that all was well. It stayed there, holding my gaze, for about five minutes. Even after the robin flew off, I simply sat there, stunned by my experience.

The rest of the day past in a haze. When I got back home, I instantly looked up what a robin Power Animal meant on the internet. No surprise that the robin's message was one of courage, hope, letting go of the old, viewing life from a different perspective and welcoming in new growth and opportunity.

Since that morning, a new world has opened up for me and set me on a new course where I have explored the gift of Power Animals in their various forms. I have come to deeply appreciate and feel grateful for their support and presence in my life.

So, for you who are reading this, I invite you to slow down, become acutely aware of your environment so that you can hear the wisdom of these truly amazing animal messengers.

Naseem Ahsun

How to Use This Book

The whole purpose of writing this book is to open a doorway to a world where you can experience your own connection with your Power Animals and access their insight and support.

In this book, I share 21 Power Animal messages and guidance, as well as ways for you to connect to your Power Animals and, should you wish it, ways for you to deepen your connection and relationship with them.

This book is by no means exhaustive, as there are always further depths and layers to be revealed and explored. Neither are the messages shared in this book the only interpretations. It is just my experience, my interpretation and my journey.

You can use this book in a number of ways to maximise your experience of Power Animals. There is no right way to use the book, so my invitation is to explore with curiosity and find what works for you.

The purpose of each section is to invite you to go within and explore aspects of yourself on a deeper level, using the Power Animals to guide and support you.

- You can simply look up a Power Animal if it appears to you by using the Power Animal Wisdom section. Here you will be able to explore the message and see how it applies to you by reflecting on the key question, as well as completing the activity to help you explore this.

- You can also use the Power Animal Wisdom section as an oracle book. Simply close your eyes and focus on asking for guidance from a Power Animal. Then thumb through the pages of this section, until you feel the urge to stop. Read the section for that Power Animal. For a deeper understanding, you might wish to reflect on the key question and complete the activity that comes with each Power Animal.

- For any Power Animals that have not been shared in this book, the invitation is for you to find your own interpretations of why they have appeared to you and do your own research.

- If you would like to meet your Power Animal, then the Power Animal guided journey will help you connect with your guide.

- Finally, if you would like to deepen your experience further, you can discover how to work with your Power Animals and your chakras.

What Are Power Animals?

As a reminder, Power Animals are guides that bring us specific messages from the Universe to help us on our life journey. They can also be life or daily companions, appearing in physical and spiritual forms. For example, your pet might be one of your Power Animals that has manifested as a physical guide. Another of your Power Animals might well come to you via other realms.

There are a number of ways we already and unconsciously tap into the natural healing abilities that animals can give us. For example, research shows that petting an animal reduces stress levels and anxiety and is often used as a therapy. Some institutions, such as prisons, use animals to cultivate trust, an open heart and compassion in their inmates. Some schools use dogs to support anxious young pupils.

Ultimately, animals have a lot to teach us about being well in ourselves, or as many call it, our wellbeing. They are natural healers who can guide and support us through all areas of our lives.

Some Power Animals will stay with us for life, whilst others will stay only for a short period of time, perhaps during a challenging time when we need that animal's energy and guidance. They can appear to us in a variety of ways and we can connect and explore them on a number of levels including: physical, emotional, mental and spiritual.

Physical
If an animal is behaving strangely, or out of character around you, then it is most likely there to give you a message.

For example, when I recently relocated, a blackbird flew into my new house on the day I moved in. It landed on the stairs and stayed there for a minute or two, nonchalantly looking around, before flying back through the front door. One meaning of a blackbird, is that it symbolises the unknown. They also herald important changes taking place, or about to take place. Very apt in my case of relocating to a new area and home.

Also, if the same animal continues to show up in your life, then it is trying to get your attention as it has a message for you. Furthermore, it will continue to show up until you listen to its message. However, this doesn't mean that you have to be hyper-vigilant, looking at every animal suspiciously, wondering if the neighbour's cat has a message for you. It is just being mindful and simply noticing when the same type of animal begins to show up in your life, where previously it hadn't.

There are a number of ways you can encounter a Power Animal: in the flesh, in an image, through your dreams - the possibilities are endless. I once remember seeing a swan, an image of a swan on a pub sign and the word swan all in the same day. Also, at the time of writing this book, whilst out and about on the first snowfall of December, a butterfly fell at my feet. Not only this, but I continued to see images of butterflies throughout the month: on jumpers, labels, wrapping paper and adverts. Butterflies signify transformation and new beginnings. They also signify the importance of process in any new business venture or project - quite significant in my case.

Emotional

If you have picked up this book, it is likely that you already feel some emotional connection to the animal kingdom. You might be a cat lover, dog lover or love animals in general. Alternatively, you might be at the other end of the spectrum – perhaps there is a specific animal that you loathe; one that causes you to freeze in fear? Many people fear spiders, for example.

I have a fear of hornets and wasps. Usually, I freeze if one flies in through the window. Yet it is through our fears that we can also gain a better understanding of ourselves and the stories we have about ourselves; stories that limit us. In the case of the hornet and wasp, who represent abundance, community, persistence, fertility and teamwork, I have discovered that these are areas I am being invited to cultivate and experience more of.

Whatever your emotional response, you are invited to explore what that means to you. If you have a fear or phobia concerning specific animals, use it as an opportunity to explore what lies beneath it.

Mental
Once you have determined your Power Animal, or you get a recurrent message from your environment about a specific animal, you can explore this animal and its characteristics by doing a little research. Read about the key characteristics, perhaps look up some stories or legends, explore the animal's environment: what it eats; how it sleeps; how it finds solutions – all these can give you insights into why it has appeared in your life and how it can support you.

There are also a number of websites that can give you further insights into Power Animals from different cultures and practices. Spend time exploring how it relates to you.

When you are next watching a wildlife

programme, consider which animals you are drawn to and which ones repel you. Draw up a list. Do you remember which animals you liked as a child? Has that changed? All these are interesting clues that can help you to determine your Power Animals, how they speak to you and how they might support you now.

Spiritual

I believe that the guidance of Power Animals can really help us in our day-to-day lives, as well as support us in connecting to the truth of who we are, which goes far beyond our personality. We are more than our thoughts, culture, background, social group or familial story. We are souls who have chosen to incarnate into a human body and experience life on Earth as human beings.

Life is uncertain, especially during the current times we live in. Consequently, the guidance of our Power Animals who walk beside us, within us, below us and above us, is doubly important. They can help us integrate all aspects of ourselves and support our embodiment of our physicality; truly embracing the gift of being ourselves.

Life continuously invites us to discover the greater capacity of ourselves: through personal challenges, loss, success; failure; relationship; in fact, all areas of our lives. This is where our Power Animals can really help us. By connecting with their energy, we gain a greater sense of intimacy and connection with ourselves, others and our environment. Whatever your query, be assured that your Power Animal will guide you to the answers which live deep within you.

POWER ANIMAL WISDOM

Tiger

Tiger energy is all about boldly stepping into the flow of life to cultivate new direction. The power of the Tiger invites you to strike out on your own, be adventurous and try something new and different. Explore the unexplored in your life and discover new aspects of yourself. Whatever area in your life you wish to explore, remember that you have all the resources you need within you to thrive. You are capable of more than you know. It is your time to journey with Tiger to discover it.

Key Question:
What have I always wanted to explore?

Activity
- For 1 week, try something new. It could be a new meal, taking a different route to work or watching a new tv show.

- Get a globe and write down all the countries or regions you would like to visit.

Antelope

Antelope is not about standing still, but for moving forward. Now is the time to act. Taking positive action will enable you to overcome obstacles and achieve your objective. Trust that you have the skills to navigate changeable situations. Be flexible and above all do not stand still, but act.

Key Question:

What is the next appropriate action I can take in the here and now?

Activity

- Go for a walk, in nature. You could try a new route or path. Alternatively, you could try a different variation of your normal walk. Consider how you have navigated the route to your destination.

- Break it down into steps and write it down. Consider whether you had to deviate. Did you take a wrong turn? Were you able to turn back?

- Now do the same for the next steps you can take regarding your issue, knowing that you can always make adjustments as you go along.

Bat

A time of rebirth and transition. When one door closes, another opens. A time of transformation and birthing a new aspect of yourself. During this process, Bat invites you to acknowledge and honour whatever emotions arise, remembering to be kind to yourself as you physically allow yourself to feel them. Then be willing to let go of those things in your life that no longer serve you. You are in the process of creating space for a new period of your life to birth.

Key Question:
What am I ready to release in my life?

Activity
- Declutter areas of your home, room or wardrobe and recycle the items you no longer need.

- Open the windows and allow the cleansing energy of air the freedom to move through your home.

- Alternatively, you can cleanse your area with incense or sage.

Panther

Draw on your own courage and enter the unknown to follow your own pathway. This is often the path less travelled and requires your ultimate trust in the process. The journey is of more importance than the destination as Panther invites you to truly BE you, rather than a watered-down version of yourself to please others. It is a journey of honesty, self-acceptance, compassion and reclamation. Panther energy supports you into tapping into your courage in the face of your fears and doubts about what truly resonates with you. By being in the now, you allow the process to unfold in all its magic and synchronicity.

Key Question:
How can I learn to tap into my courage in the face of the unknown?

Suggested Activity
- For the next five days make a list of your fears that arise during each day.

- At the end of the five days, identify which fears are current and which fears are old and which fears are based in the future.

- How do you feel when you drop the fears that do not apply in the here and now?

Hawk

Listen intently to the whispers on the wind for the messages that will come to you from your environment, the Universe and others who cross your path. Embrace different viewpoints and take a step back to see the bigger picture. Be the observer or witness to the situations and people around you; use your inner sight – your insight - and intuition to help bring focus to what is really happening beneath the surface. You are also invited to focus on what needs to be done in the here and now to complete a task.

Key Question:
How open am I to listening to viewpoints that differ from my own?

Activity
- The next time you are in conversation, notice how often you mentally agree or disagree with a person based on your views about a subject.

- Try reading a book upside down, sideways, upright – which are you most comfortable with?

- Break big projects down into little steps and focus on completing each one.

Wolf

Wolf is a powerful teacher if you are open to the guidance that is given. Wolf can teach you many lessons, whether it is from your immediate environment, your studies or other people. Look for the teacher and the learning in all that you encounter. Trust this powerful ally and learn all there is to learn about your environment. Wolf acts as the pathfinder and invites you to open yourself to new learning and developing new skills. This will help you to move forward.

Key Question:
How open am I to new learning and developing my skills and abilities?

Activity
- If you are right handed, learn to use your left hand when writing or brushing your teeth. Notice how easy or hard it is. Notice how long it takes. Spend a week or two practising this new skill.

- How does it make you feel?

- Next consider any new skill that will be helpful in your job, personal life or one you've always wanted to learn.

Salmon

Salmon goes with the flow, trusting its inner knowing and inner-guidance system. Through inner-knowing, you touch upon your own inner-wisdom, even in the midst of others' judgement. Rather than blindly following others, or relying on them to provide the answers, it is time to go deep within yourself and trust that your inner-knowing will act as the best guide through any situation. You already know what needs to be done.

Key Question:

How often do I trust my inner-gut and inner-knowing?

Activity

- Connect with your inner-knowing by using this visualisation:

  Find a place where you will not be disturbed. Turn off all social media and phones. You can sit or lie down.

  Take three breaths through your nose and out through your mouth. As you exhale, release all tension, feel new energy flow into you as you inhale.

  Now, follow your breath to your gut. Really breathe into your belly, into your digestive system. Feel the area expand with each new breath. Feel it awaken to new energy.

  How does it feel? What colour is it?

- Note down what you experienced in the visualisation.

- Next time you are faced with a choice or feel confused, connect with your gut through your breath and notice how it feels.

Crow

Crow is a shapeshifter with the power of intuition and is a symbol of Universal Law. It invites you to question what you believe to be true in light of the bigger picture. Look beyond your limited thinking to explore beyond what you know, or think you know. It is also the omen of change and surrender to something greater than yourself. You are called to act in honour in all that you do; walk your talk. For you to truly succeed, you are challenged to go beyond your limited view of yourself and others – only by moving beyond limitation and being open to new possibilities can you truly discover the magic.

Key Question:
How does my sense of identity limit my experiences?

Activity
- Volunteer your time in your community–
  whether it be for an organisation or helping
  a neighbour.

- Make a list of everything you know,
  everything you don't know and everything
  you don't know that you don't know. What
  do you notice?

Dolphin

The power of Dolphin brings you the power of play and fun to provide wellness in your life. Naturally sociable, amiable and communicative, Dolphin invites you to join the party. Through actively engaging in fun activities with no purpose other than to enjoy, you will naturally flow back into alignment with yourself and your life. By aligning to your needs, you will create space for rest, relaxation and work. Consequently, you will feel a greater sense of wellness, greater productivity, increased resilience in dealing with challenges and experience more joy in your life.

Key Question:
How often do I take time out to play?

Activity
- Take a morning out of your week to do something for fun.

- For the next month, take an hour out of your day for simple relaxation.

- Observe what children do for fun.

- Watch a program about dolphins, or go and observe dolphins in the wild.

- Plan a fun, group activity with friends.

Swan

Swan represents the power of grace and surrender. By accepting and acknowledging whatever is taking place, rather than resisting it, or seeking to control it, you open yourself up to transformation. This process of surrender and grace is one of complete acceptance in whatever is unfolding in your life and a deep trust that the Universe is supporting you through this. Swan represents living in partnership with the Universe.

Key Question:
What am I resisting?

Activity

- Write ten sentences starting with *I don't like...* and complete the statement based on what is happening in your life.

- Which of the *I don't like* statements can you drop?

- Spend the day noticing the amount of times you or others use the word, *I should/they should.*

Eagle

The wings of Eagle connect you to your consciousness and awareness. Eagle soars high into these realms, where you are able to connect to the Universe. Trust the messages and intuitions that come to you as Eagle seeks to help you gain an overview of what is occurring in your life and current situation. You are invited to soar above the jigsaw puzzle. By doing this, you will gain a more objective viewpoint where you will find clarity and your answers.

Key Question:
How can I take a step back when I feel confused or overwhelmed?

Activity
- Go to a high place somewhere in nature like a cliff or a hill. If you can't access nature, then find a tall building, even the first floor of your house and just watch the world go by. Notice how clearly you can see when you step back to look at the bigger picture.

- What can you see from this view that others, who are down on the ground, cannot see?

- Complete a jigsaw puzzle. Notice how the chaotic and confusing image comes together through your patient perseverance.

Heron

Deeply reflective, the Heron invites you to go inwards and digest the events that are flowing through your life. Heron looks beyond the surface of things, and when it is ready, it strikes quickly and with precision. So, it invites you to be reflective about your actions, your circumstances, going beyond the surface to explore the patterns and behaviours that drive your actions and have brought you to your present place. Taking time to process events gives you an opportunity to gain a greater awareness of yourself and your story. It is an invitation to slow down, dive deep into the waters of Heron and begin to notice patterns and behaviours, without judgement, that have created your present circumstances.

Key Question:
What patterns do I notice in my life?

Activity
- Go for a swim and notice the difference between going underwater and swimming on the surface.

- Look at yourself in a bowl of water or mirror – now try and see beneath the surface. Write down what you notice.

Butterfly

A powerful symbol of transformation. New beginnings are at hand and will move you forward to positive growth. A step-by-step approach is needed for success, so do not miss steps and remember the importance of process, particularly when setting up your own business, or entering into a new project. It is a journey of exploration, one to be savoured, so give yourself permission to enjoy it. There is no need to rush. In fact, being in step with each unfolding moment and natural timing will bring you exactly what you need.

Key Question:
How do I view new beginnings?

Activity

- Explore the metamorphosis and journey of a caterpillar. Journal what you notice.

- Explore birth – from the birth of the Universe to the birth of a child – what do you notice?

- Consider the cycles of the year and the cycle that fruit trees go through each year. Note down what you notice.

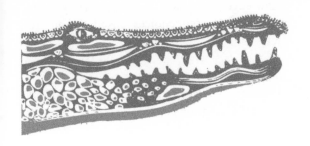

Crocodile

A need for integration is at hand if Crocodile has crossed your path. This ancient Power Animal has honed its instincts over thousands of years to become a master of its environment. Its timing is perfect. It will be absolutely still whilst it gathers the information it needs from its environment. Once gathered, Crocodile will utilise it and move swiftly and confidently toward its prize. Consequently, Crocodile invites you to use all your senses to discern all aspects of a specific situation occurring in your life. This means that you need to gather as much factual information as you can before you can make your move. Coming from this knowledgeable place will support you in making grounded choices based on all the facts.

Key Question:
How can I make grounded choices when faced with a challenge or possibility?

Activity
- Take an orange or tangerine and look at its shape. Next feel it's skin. Write down what you notice. Now smell it and write down what you smell. Next begin to peel it. Notice the sound it makes and how it feels to peel it. Describe the layer beneath – what do you see? How does it feel? Break the orange or tangerine into segments. What shape is it? Now, take a piece of the fruit and place it in your mouth. How does it feel? Finally, bite into it and taste it. Write down your findings.
- Create a who, what, where, when, why, how template to help you explore any particular challenge or possibility in your life.
- Create a list of questions about the challenges and possibilities you are currently facing.

Snake

Snake Power Animal provides healing and transformative medicine which takes place deep within you. You are invited to shed your old skin of past hurts and betrayals so that they cease having power over you in the here and now. Only through the acceptance and acknowledgment of your pain can you look to transcend it and move forward to new pastures and a different way of being. Snake is the power of the healer within you and invites you to stop warring with yourself, your past, your future. It is a lesson of total surrender to what is. By surrendering to what is, or what was, you begin the journey of forgiving – meaning **for giving** life energy back to yourself and to others.

Key Question:
What is ready to be healed in my life?

Activity
- Begin an internal visualised scan of your body. Close your eyes and start at your feet. Go within and sense the energy of your feet. Next, slowly move up to your ankles, legs, knees, then work your way up through the rest of your body until you reach the crown of your head. Notice where you feel pain (physical, emotional) then stop. Go a little deeper into the pain, tracking it right back to the source. Notice what happens as you take the time to really connect and acknowledge the pain.

- Watch a video on how a snake sheds it skin. What do you notice?

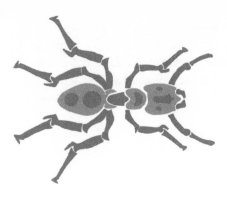

Ant

The power of patience, perseverance and persistence lies at the centre of the Ant Power Animal. To access this Power Animal, is to access the secret of building strong foundations. Although seemingly insignificant, this small insect and its qualities can move mountains, especially through cooperation and teamwork. The art of patience and trusting as you consistently and diligently apply yourself to a project, enterprise or task is what is called for. Remember that what is yours will always come to you, so do not let a fear of missing out cause you to hurry or feel anxious. Trust that you will get there in spite of any detours, which are a blessing in disguise. If your first attempts fail or you get stuck, persist, for failure and being stuck invites you to take a detour, so you can discover new pathways that will widen your experience and bring you the success you seek.

Key Question:
How do I build strong foundations?

Activity
- Explore how an Ant's nest is constructed and look at how ants behave and work together as a team to create strong foundations.

- Explore the internal structure of the body and look at how the skeleton supports the body.

- Look at the foundations needed to build a house.

Tortoise

The art of grounding and slowing down is central to the Tortoise's gift. You are invited to connect with the Earth, your reality, your environment and current time. Slow down and rediscover your body's natural rhythm and get back into step with yourself. This Power Animal is all about pacing yourself, making sure that you are taking care of yourself and your needs. Move too fast and there is the risk of rash decisions and paths that lead to dead ends, as well as injury. Take regular time out and check in on yourself and your energy levels.

Key Question:
Do I take the time to fulfil my personal needs?

Activity
- Take time to go for a walk and walk at half your usual pace.

- Each day take twenty minutes to simply sit quietly, doing nothing.

- Take your time when eating. Slow down and savour your food; really chew, smell and feel the different textures and flavours.

Spider

The creative web of Spider encourages you to explore your own creativity. Creativity is the Universe at work within you and invites you to express yours. It enables you to access your own inner-gifts and share them with the world. Far from being a waste of time, getting creative when you are stuck helps you access solutions that are outside of your current awareness. Through creativity you can untangle problems, open yourself up to new opportunities and possibilities that will help you move through challenges in your life. It is a reminder that you are a creative being.

Key Question:
How can creativity help me develop new solutions to existing problems?

Activity
- Cook a new meal one evening.

- Take up Art or a new hobby.

- Explore the design of a spider's web and consider the geometry that helps it to capture its prey.

- Write a story or poem.

Deer

The gentleness of Deer invites you to embrace all aspects of love and allow its energy and power to work through you. Deer is all about kindness and unconditional love; to yourself and others. It's all about loving yourself and others just as you and they are. There is no need to change yourself, or try to change others to fit your idea of perfection. The focus on self-improvement can take you further away from yourself, increasing your belief and suffering of not being good enough, beautiful enough, slim enough or clever enough. Remember that you are perfect just as you are. Shifting your focus on all there is to love about yourself, others and your life can help you centre yourself and create a supportive space where you can truly embrace the amazing being that you are, as well as appreciating others.

Key Question:
How loving am I to myself and others?

Activity

- Write a love letter to yourself and post it.

- Take regular time out to have a massage or pamper yourself– notice the sensations in your body.

- Notice how you speak about yourself when you make a mistake or fail – is this similar to how you speak or think about others?

- Carry out a kind deed for someone else. How does this make you feel?

- Volunteer your time. How does this make you feel?

Horse

Horse Power Animal speaks of true power and your ability to direct your power in the real world. Horse will carry you toward your own centre of power that resides deep inside you and it is all about how you empower yourself in your life. You are reminded that you are a powerful being and you can use your power in ways that benefit you or limit you. You can use your power to empower yourself and others, or disempower yourself and others. It is your choice as to how you use it, particularly in relationships at: work, home and with family. It is also about stamina and the power to stay a course; endurance in the face of challenge and using power to move you forward. Whichever way you choose to use it, it will have a significant impact.

Key Question:
What does power and having power mean to me?

Activity
- Go for a horse ride and notice how the horse uses its physical power.

- Scan your body and note down where you feel stronger and where you lack strength.

- Explore the art of Tai Chi or Yoga.

Dragon

Dragon Power Animal is very old and full of ancient wisdom. If Dragon has come to you today, you are invited to explore the magic of your life and learn to see it with new eyes. Look with the eyes of Dragon and you will be more able to identify the treasures that make up your life. Your very own treasure trove is full of your power, wisdom and personal magnificence. This Power Animal is also one of protection and invites you to access your courage in the face of adversity; tap into inspiration to lead you out of difficulty and step into your leadership.

Ultimately, you are asked to acknowledge and value the gifts you have always possessed.

Key Question:
What are the treasures I already possess?

Activity
- Create your own image of a dragon – What is it called? Is it male, female, neither? What are its gifts? What treasure does it seek? How does this represent you?

- Research the mythology of dragons from different cultures.

- Create an abundance tree and list the treasure you own – it is not just material things, but also family, friends, time, health etc.

Meet Your Power Animal

If you've ever wanted to know who your Power Animal is, then you will need to journey to them to discover who they are and how they can assist you in your own life. Your Power Animal isn't one that you choose either; it is they who choose you. You might be very surprised as to who they are. This is something I discovered during my own journey to connect with my Power Animal. Ultimately, your Power Animal is the one who will best serve you in that moment in time. They might have key characteristics or traits similar to your own. Alternatively, they might have different qualities that you are invited to explore.

Your Power Animal might also be one that doesn't appear in this book, yet you can explore them in ways suggested in the *What are Power Animals?* section of the book.

To meet your Power Animal, you will need to journey to the lower world. In Shamanism, there are three worlds: lower world, middle world and upper world. The lower world is where nature spirits reside: from Power Animals, plant allies, and other energies of Nature. The middle world represents our everyday physical world that we live in, whilst the upper world is where we connect with universal consciousness, angels, our spirit guides and teachers.

To connect to the lower world to meet your Power Animal, you will need to create your own imaginary portal or entrance.

1. First make sure the space you will be doing your journey is private (where you will not be disturbed for the next half hour) comfortably warm and cleansed. You can cleanse your space using sage or incense. Also, mentally set your intention as you cleanse the room thoroughly. You can do this by stating what you will be using the space for e.g. *I cleanse this space with the intention of journeying to find my Power Animal. You should repeat this at least 3 times.*

2. Before you close your eyes, take careful note of the room you are in, noticing all

there is to notice about it. Make sure you have a glass of water ready for when you finish.

3.   You will need to be seated with your feet close to the ground. You can sit cross-legged if you so wish.

4.   Begin by becoming aware of all of your body, scanning from your feet through to the crown of your head. Look around the room and be aware of all that is in it.

5.   Now, close your eyes, take three deep inhalations through your nose and down to your feet. With each exhale, feel yourself releasing the tensions of the day.

6.   Next, imagine your feet growing roots that go through the floor, through the crust of the earth below until it reaches the core of the Earth. Feel the Earth's energy reaching up through the roots into your body.

7.   In your mind's eye imagine a place in nature that is untouched and appealing to you. This can be anywhere in nature that you have created in your imagination: it could be a cave, an island, a beach, meadow, mountain top, forest – wherever seems safe and pleasant to you.   Imagine this

space in as much detail as you can. What you can see, hear, feel, touch and smell? Explore your surroundings, and as you explore, you notice an opening. You move toward the opening, watching it grow in size as you draw nearer. It is big enough to step through, which you do. As you step through, you notice yourself descending through a tunnel, which takes you deep into the Earth: deeper into the rock and crystals, until you reach the bottom where another opening appears before you.

8. As you step toward the opening, you find yourself in another natural environment – take a moment to notice what it is like. Where is it? What is the weather like? What is the temperature? What do you notice about the details?

9. Now walk into this environment and begin to explore. As you continue to walk, use your senses to see, feel, hear, taste, touch and sense.

10. As you continue to walk you begin to sense that you are not alone. You might see a number of animals around you. Some might come and go, whilst others

may show up more than once. When you notice the same animal three times, then you know that you are meeting your Power Animal.

11. Take some time to examine this animal, what does it look like? What colour is it? What is it doing?

12. When you are ready, approach the animal respectfully and communicate with it. Ask it why it has appeared to you and wait for the answer. You might have other questions for it too. Ask it if it is willing to be your guide. If it is, then thank it and hold out your hand. As you do, you will see your Power Animal either shrink or transform itself in some way so that its energy becomes part of your own.

13. Now, make your way back to the entrance and take the tunnel back up. Feel yourself coming back to where you started. Leave the entrance and make your way back to yourself in the room that you are in. Feel yourself in your body by taking in three inhalations, inhaling right down to your feet. With each inhalation and exhalation, feel yourself more present in your body.

Feel yourself more present in the room. Visualise the detail of the room in your mind's eye. When you are ready, open your eyes. Take a moment to look around the room, taking note of everything you see.

14. Move your toes and fingers to physically ground yourself. And when you are ready, get up and move around.

15. Take your time to drink your glass of water.

16. Make a note of your journey, who your Power Animal is, what they shared with you and anything else you feel of importance in the journey. If you can, draw an image of them, noting the colours and the environment.

Once you know who your Power Animal is, it is important that you find ways to honour them and build a relationship with them. For example, creating pieces of art of your Power Animal, meditating on your animal, or simply acknowledging their presence with thanks and gratitude at the end of each day will help to maintain the bond.

Now that you have met with your Power Animal, you will be able to establish regular contact with them by simply visualising their presence – they may or may not have a message for you. However, feeling their energy in and around you will help support you in certain situations. You might want to keep a journal of your findings, meetings and messages as it will help develop your relationship with your Power Animal.

Dance and Your Power Animal

A wonderful and powerful way to connect with your Power Animal and really embody its energy is to dance your Power Animal. This tradition goes back thousands of years and was used by our ancestors to invoke the energy of a particular animal. There is no right or wrong way to do this, as it is all about the intention.

Dance has been a powerful tool for transformation and releasing of energy in many cultures and has been used by indigenous cultures such as the Navajo, Zulu and Maori for thousands of years. It is another way for us to embody our bodies. When we are dancing our Power Animals, we really begin to feel a deeper connection with them and the wisdom they can teach us.

I once remember meeting one of my Power Animals in just such a fashion during an Ecstatic Awakening Dance, which is a deeply transformational dance and active meditation. Whilst deep in the dance, Panther came clawing out of my deepest recesses, right from my roots, up through my throat and roaring out of my mouth. Suddenly I was she and she was me, a part of me I had repressed for years. I was so shocked by her ferocity, yet exhilarated as I felt her energy, her sense of primordial power. I felt a wholeness and fierceness that I hadn't felt before. It was almost as if she was daring me to BE me. That evening I accessed emotions and parts of myself I never knew existed – and it was during that evening that I really felt like I was coming home to me.

You too can feel a closer link and gain further insight into your Power Animal through the timeless power of dance.

You might well ask, 'How do I do this?'

1. You might want to find somewhere private, where you won't be disturbed.
2. Next set your intention and mentally invite your Power Animal to dance with you.
3. Choose music with a tribal beat and when you are ready, really begin to visualise

how your animal moves and mimic those movements.

4. It might feel mechanical at first, but as you continue to really embody your animal, you will find the flow. You might even end up sounding like your animal. The trick is to give your body free reign in this process as it does not involve your programmed brain.

5. You might also feel all sorts of feelings and emotions coming through you via your animal: it could be anger, freedom, sadness, joy, passion. Whatever it is, simply allow it to be. Feel it! Dance it! Express it!

6. Your animal could bring you a message via the dance.

7. Keep up your dance for as long as you can, no less than 20 minutes.

8. Once your dance is complete, journal about your experience and remember to thank your Power Animal for being with you.

The Chakras
and Power Animals

What are Chakras?

Chakras are energy centres that exist within our bodies. Each chakra serves a specific function that supports us in our health and wellbeing. Our chakras also offer us a vast amount of information about our physical, emotional, mental and spiritual health.

Although we have many chakras within us, the seven basic chakras are the ones we will be focusing on in this book.

Our seven chakras connect us to the roots of the Earth, helping us stay connected to this world. They also reach all the way up toward the cosmos and the Universe, like the trunk of a tree. We are, in effect, a bridge between the Divine and material plane.

The seven chakras include the:

- Root chakra;
- Sacral chakra;
- Solar Plexus chakra;
- Heart chakra;
- Throat chakra;
- Third eye chakra;
- Crown chakra.

Each of the seven chakras are located at specific points on our body, starting at the base of our spine with the Root chakra.

Each chakra has a specific purpose and provides information about aspects of our Being and life force. As we experience life in all its multifaceted forms, so too does it affect us, which then directly impacts our chakras. Consequently, we feel the effect on all levels: physical, mental, emotional and spiritual. For example, there might be days when you feel full of energy, then days where you can hardly drag yourself out of bed. You might have periods of sickness or periods of confusion, where you can't seem to think straight. At times, you might feel especially agitated or excited. Some refer to this impact on our chakras as being blocked or unbalanced.

You might be familiar with chakras and heard about unblocking or balancing your chakras. However, there is another possibility: a gift to be found in the blocked or unbalanced energy of your chakras. It can be an indication that you are either outside of your comfort zone or are holding onto something that does not serve you – almost like a resistance. Whichever it is, you are most certainly being given a great opportunity to explore it, as it is a message that something within is asking you to notice it.

In addition, each chakra can affect the other. For example, if you're feeling low or depressed, the issue might stem from a Root chakra issue. Are you going through family disruption? Do you feel uneasy or anxious about being able to support yourself with a job, house or money? It is important to remember that each part of our body is designed to work in harmony with the other. Your body is like a giant orchestra and you are the conductor of the music of your life. When you hear a note of discord, it is a sign to notice it and explore beneath the surface.

Yet, far too often, people are desperate for balance, usually because they feel so uncomfortable and vulnerable when they are not. So, rather than allow themselves to experience their imbalance, they suppress it, as they have been taught it is not ok to be out of balance. But the truth is that, to be human is to live in the gift of both balance and imbalance, of ebb and flow, of detours and dead ends. It is through these imbalances and blocks that we are able to grow beyond what we know or think we know.

With the desperation to be 'spiritual' and our idea of this super perfect being, we have really missed the real gift here, which is our humanity. It is in our humanity that our perfection exists, including all our 'apparent' flaws. It is here, in our humanity, where we can access our ability for compassion; for healing; for non-judgement; for witnessing and noticing; for feeling the richness of emotions; to feel our capacity for love and forgiveness; to experience our darkest emotions; our fear and our self-doubt.

If we only take time to integrate the parts that we deem worthy or acceptable, we never really get to explore our true potential and our gifts. We are already spiritually aware as spirits in our human body, and we are already Divine. Yet it is the gift of humanity that we are here to experience and embody, not the other way around! That is where our true genius lies. And, we do not have to do this alone. The Universe has given us allies to support us; one of them being our Power Animals.

Accessing Your Power Animals Thorough the Chakras

Within each chakra, we can draw upon the wisdom and guidance of Power Animals to support us on our inner exploration. These willing helpers and supporters can help us find our own solutions and guide us back to ourselves.

This journey of integration can bring us face-to-face with aspects of ourselves that we might not even be aware of, aspects which we might have rejected or kept under lock and key. Yet in acknowledging that aspect of us without judging, begins the most powerful journey of forgiveness – giving ourselves back to us – disentangling ourselves from illusion, delusions and into a more honest relationship with ourselves and a more enriched one with our outer world too.

So, in this next section, we will be exploring each chakra, how it operates on a physical, emotional, mental and spiritual level. At the end of the chakra descriptions, you will be given a chakra Power Animal journey exercise, so that you can connect with the Power Animal that can best serve you in exploring that chakra and discover more of yourself in the process. Remember that you cannot do this wrong and whichever Power Animal you find to support you with exploring a particular chakra, will be the right one for you. If the Power Animal is not in this book, then you will need to do your own research.

You can do the journey a number of times over the years. You might even find that the Power Animal changes, depending on what is happening in your life at the time. You might wish to keep a journal, or record it in a way that resonates with you.

Root Chakra

Location:	Base of the spine at the tailbone
Colour:	Red
Physical:	Hips, legs, lower back, genitals, feet
Emotional:	Safety, security, resources, grounded, fear, anxiety, insecurity
Mental:	Family values, beliefs, reality, relationship to mother
Spiritual:	Manifestation, birth, ancestral line

The Root chakra is all about the physical realm, how supported we feel as we explore the physical world we live in. It is concerned with survival and fulfilling the basic human needs such as food, shelter and safety. In addition, it is about manifestation, using the Root chakra energy to bring things into the physical world. This could be birthing something new, like a child, business or project. It is linked to the element of Earth and also represents core family beliefs from which our core programming stems from, as well as the programming offered by our cultural and religious heritage – here is where it all takes root as it offers us a sense of security i.e. what is known and predictable.

It is also the energy that teaches us about building from the ground up. For example, when starting any new project, whether personal or business, it is important to put the foundations and building blocks in place to ensure secure growth. This often requires careful research, fact-finding and making sure that the details are taking care of. When these foundations or roots are planted deeply, it offers a feeling of safety in the face of the unknown.

When we experience anxiety, insecurity, agitation, fear or frustration, or feel unsafe in the world, worrying about issues of security, providing for ourselves and our family, it is reflected in this energy centre, which becomes sluggish. This could be due to a number of reasons. We might ask the following questions: Have I expanded too quickly without setting foundations? Have I missed a step in my rush or fear to get to the end? Do I feel ungrounded, as if I don't belong?

Ultimately, the gifts of this chakra, is about slow and steady building blocks, rather than rushing ahead, hence why its movements are the slowest of all the chakras.

We are invited to nurture our intention as a mother would its child, giving it the care, energy and space it needs to grow.

Sacral Chakra

Location:	Pelvis, womb
Colour:	Orange
Physical:	Reproductive system and sexual organs, bladder, kidneys, urinary tract
Emotional:	Joy, pleasure, release, orgasm
Mental:	Creativity, fun
Spiritual:	Wellbeing, abundance

The Sacral Chakra sits a little higher than the Root chakra and is your feeling centre, as well as your centre of creativity. It is where we process and feel our deepest emotions of joy, sexuality, pleasure and can feel the world around us using all of our senses.

Accessing pleasure and fun out of life is central to our wellbeing and it is through this chakra that we access our desire to create and connect with others, as well as the world around us.

This chakra is all about movement and supports our flexibility and our ability to enter into the flow of life, especially allowing the flow of emotions. By feeling our emotions, it allows us to process and release them. It is the place where we nurture ourselves and our relationships. It is also where we take pleasure in the world around us.

When we repress our feelings, ignore our need for self-nurture and fun, this chakra can become stagnant or blocked. It might manifest in the form of addictions as a temporary relief. It might manifest as feeling unable to climb out of sadness or anger. Yet if we are uncomfortable with feeling our emotions, we might try to replace it or cover it up with another emotion.

Isn't it funny how we judge emotions as either good or bad, negative or positive? And we believe that we need to be positive all the time, so we suppress emotions we judge to be negative by not allowing ourselves to feel them. Yet, ironically, this ensures that they stick around for longer; sometimes days - sometimes years.

One thing I have learnt in my own personal journey is that you cannot force your emotions to change: you can only repress or suppress them, which in my case, manifests into comfort eating. However, once you give yourself permission to feel your emotion without judging it as good or bad, negative or positive, or try to fix it, you allow it to move through you and out of you. It might take a moment, a day or longer. The point is that this chakra helps emotion move through you – it is in the very word, emotion, which means energy in motion; that is what emotions are. It is only our human tendency to judge them as good or bad, positive or negative that prevents us from feeling them.

Solar Plexus Chakra

Location:	Upper part of your belly, where your diaphragm rests
Colour:	Yellow
Physical:	The respiratory system and diaphragm, digestive system, stomach, liver, gallbladder, kidney, pancreas, adrenal glands, spleen, the small intestine, the lower back, the sympathetic nervous system
Emotional:	Self-esteem, confidence, assertiveness, power, pride, shame
Mental:	Taking action
Spiritual:	Relationship with yourself and others, empowerment

Here lies the seat of our power; our will and our assertiveness. It is also the centre where our core personality and ego lies and is, what I call, the action chakra – energy moving in the 3D world and how we assert and use our power in it.

From this place, we can access the energy to put ideas and plans into action. We can respond to our environment, or react to our environment dependent on how we view power and ourselves. It is a manifestation of how we access our power, as well as how we use our power to move us forward, or to limit us and others.

This chakra invites us to take responsibility for where we are in our lives and to recognise that we always have a choice as to how we use our power, or how we choose not to use our power. When we are in alignment and centred in ourselves, we feel more confident, motivated and empowered to fulfil our goals. When we are off centre, or out of alignment, we might feel pride, stubbornness, a need for control, lack of motivation and lack confidence.

If we are afraid of power, or judge it as negative, we might feel an imbalance here, or feel blocked and powerless. If so, then some questions to consider are: Where do I feel weak or helpless? Where do I feel powerless? What am I reacting to? Where do I blame others? What am I resisting?

Another thing to consider is when we over-stimulate our Solar Plexus chakra by being too goal-orientated, or push ahead by imposing our need for control. For example, have you ever moved ahead believing that you can push through obstacles with your determination and willpower alone? This is certainly something that is promoted in modern society today: that just by using and directing your power of will, you can manifest what you want. This has often led to blinkered vision, depletion and burn out. It is a complete misunderstanding of the secret of manifestation.

One other important aspect to consider with this chakra is that it is where your gut instinct resides: in your stomach. It is the only other part of your body to contain the grey cell matter of your brain and, consequently, acts like your second brain. Therefore, it has a direct line of communication to the crown chakra, the chakra that connects to universal power and the power of the Universe. You might have heard of going with your gut or gut instinct, which can be translated into communication from the Universe. It is experienced as a sense of instinctual knowing, more commonly known as intuition. Dependent on how much you trust your power centre, this can come as a whisper, a sensation or a resounding clarion. On a purely instinctual level and physical level, you might well have felt it respond to danger or potential danger. For example, how does it feel when someone makes you jump?

Ultimately, the gift of this chakra, is your ability to impact the world through the actions you choose to take.

Heart Chakra

Location:	Centre of the chest
Colour:	Green
Physical:	Heart, circulatory system, lungs, hands, arms, back
Emotional:	Love, grief, trust, compassion, kindness, empathy, intimacy, healthy boundaries, gratitude, self-acceptance and self-love, honesty, jealousy, envy, forgiveness.
Mental:	Sociable, open, balance of emotions and logic
Spiritual:	Interconnectedness, inner-peace, integration, completeness, humanitarian, altruistic, service, selflessness, healing

The Heart chakra acts as a bridge from our physical bodies to the Universe. It is also the place of self-love. From this place of self-love and self-acceptance of who we are, without judgement or condemnation, we discover the power of being self-centred, which means being centred in ourselves. From this place of harmony, we find ourselves in direct alignment with our world and with the Universe, with open hearts.

When our hearts are open, we are open to receiving from the Universe and each other. When we are open, it is easy to access support, solutions, opportunities, love, kindness, compassion, abundance and joy. When we are open, it is easy to recognise our need for healthy boundaries, so we can continue to treat ourselves lovingly.

However, when our Heart chakra is closed or off centre, we might feel a lack of trust, fear that we are not loveable, or believe that we are not deserving. It might be that out of this belief of being unlovable, we have a tendency to say yes to things and other people even when we don't want to because of our fear of being disliked. We might also feel a lack of trust in relationships and experience jealousy or envy, as a result.

From this place, we begin to isolate ourselves and armour ourselves against others, against life and against the Universe. We also armour ourselves against ourselves, meaning that we might find it difficult or impossible to accept certain parts of ourselves due to our judgements. Consequently, we deny that they are even there, or reject these aspects of ourselves we feel ashamed about. This often results in us presenting the world with the parts we want them to see. Therefore, the way we experience life, ourselves and our relationships is surface level, lacking the depth of true intimacy.

This chakra, that sits in our centre, is a doorway through which we can access deeper levels of ourselves and is the gateway to our happiness and wellbeing. This doesn't mean the trappings of the world or achieving goals. It is more about our inner state of wellbeing, being well in ourselves, who we are and how kind we are to ourselves. How kind we are to ourselves is a great indicator of how kind we are to others, as well as how we connect with them.

It is also here that our relationship with money, abundance and prosperity becomes clearer. Do you trust that you will be provided for, that solutions will come and that you are supported? If trust is hard to come by, we can sometimes compensate by overstimulating our Solar Plexus chakra by trying to control outcomes so that we do get those things, rather than trust that what is meant for us will always find its way home.

Ultimately, to have an open heart is to be truly vulnerable so that you might experience the joy of intimacy and magical relationships: with yourself, others and the Universe.

Throat Chakra

Location: Neck and Shoulders
Colour: Sky Blue/Aquamarine
Physical: Neck, throat, thyroid, lymphatic
                system, mouth, teeth, arms,
                shoulders, hands, vocal chords,
                breath, ears
Emotional: Truth, creativity, manifestation,
                congruent, manipulative, dishonest,
Mental: Communication, speech, influence,
                self-expression, silence
Spiritual: Inner-truth, authentic voice,
                connection, life

The Throat chakra is the space for our self-expression and communication to the world and with ourselves. It is the space where we give expression from all of our other chakras too. For example, our emotions, our love, our anger, our opinion, our assertiveness, our fear, our beliefs and our dreams. It is how we communicate our reality and experiences, as well as how we seek to connect with others.

Through the Throat chakra, what has been kept in the dark can be brought out into the light. It is the chakra that is increasingly dominating our human lives, whether it be: speaking, writing, singing, humming, silence, music, art, our thoughts. It has the power to influence, manifest and most directly make real whatever is gestating and requiring expression within us. We can even see it through our technologies: the internet and the rise of social media connects us on the global web of communication, which dominates our modern society.

The gift of this chakra is also in our ability to listen and truly hear what others are communicating by keeping ourselves open to what they are saying and how they are feeling. This can be challenging to us, as we have all grown proficient at expressing, rather than developing the ability to listen and hear others clearly.

The power of the Throat chakra is immense and it has a direct impact on cause and effect.

We are creative beings who are constantly creating our reality. We literally breathe life into our creations through how we self-express, as well as what we self-express.

We all affect each other and our environment through our speech patterns. When our Throat chakra is open, we express in an honest, open way. However, if we fear to give voice to what we really think or feel, then our Throat chakra becomes armoured, which directly impacts our ability to give voice to what we are really thinking or feeling. Consider what we choose to express? Or what we choose not to express? What do we fear to express? At times, silence is an even more powerful form of self-expression.

Third Eye Chakra

Location:	Between the eyebrows
Colour:	Indigo
Physical:	Eyes, frontal lobe, penal gland, ears, nose, nervous system, pituitary gland
Emotional:	Emotional intelligence, understanding
Mental:	Imagination, Inspiration, Illusion, perspective, viewpoint, focus
Spiritual:	Insight, clear-seeing, intuition, self-awareness, wisdom

The Third Eye chakra has most commonly been known as the psychic centre – the place where we can learn to develop our psychic abilities. However, it is much more than that; it is the place where we begin to connect to our universal potential and the Universe itself, as well as developing our insight – our ability to see within.

It is from this space and wheel of energy that we connect with our inner-vision, which operates like a guide during our human journey. When our Third Eye is open we open to the universal intelligence of the Universe, we can see clearly and discern between illusion and reality. With this chakra we are able to see beyond what we know, or think we know and become aware of more than we can see in the physical world. It is as if we gain a second-sight, which is a common term used to describe clairvoyance. We see all that is hidden. For some, this manifests as a seeing beyond the physical world. Ultimately, it is the ability to see beyond the obvious; to gain an understanding of the multiple spectrums of colour and viewpoints between black and white.

It is also here that we begin to gain closer contact with the unseen world of spirit; we might be given guidance through our dreams or have premonitions; we might experience something more direct.

As we open our Third Eye, so we open our vision to possibilities we might not have considered before. Although we might not know how these possibilities will unfold, it is more in receiving the message of these possibilities where the gift lies. Once received, we can choose to explore or not.

Our Third Eye is also where our focus develops and our ability to choose what we focus on. Recently, I saw an experiment conducted with young people in a school. They were given a surprise test by their teacher and the test consisted of a small black spot on a piece of paper, which they were asked to write about. The teacher took the papers in and marked them. When she gave the papers back, her feedback noted that while all the answers were detailed and comprehensive, they only focused on the black dot. Not one of her students had explored the expansive white around it. Their answers were a reflection of their narrow viewpoint.

This reminds me of a painting I once saw in the Tate Gallery in London. I was 18 at the time and remember staring, aghast, at this piece of art which consisted of just such a dot. At the time, my focus was on the dot and I was disgusted by this thing that was supposedly called 'art'. How could a black dot be art? This has puzzled me for years and it is only in writing this section, that I have gained an insight into that painting and what it was inviting me to see and notice about myself, nearly thirty years later!

When our Third Eye is closed or armoured, there might be times when we only focus on what we wish to see, or what we are comfortable with seeing. As a consequence, our vision is limited by our capacity to look at life and our world from perspectives or viewpoints that are different from our own. We tend to see the world from a one-dimensional perspective based on our experience and what we know – our truth. Consequently, we might find it difficult to understand and relate to others whose experiences and truth differs from our own.

Ultimately, the Third Eye chakra invites us to step outside of what we know and what we think we know, to access the vastness of the unknown. We are invited to recognise that what we know, is a little microscopic black dot in the vastness of space.

Crown Chakra

Location:	Top of the head
Colour:	White/deep purple
Physical:	Nervous system, pineal gland, pituitary gland, skin, cerebral cortex
Emotional:	Ecstasy, wholeness, completeness
Mental:	Relationship to father, self-knowledge, to know
Spiritual:	Consciousness, universe, soul, unity, enlightenment

The Crown chakra is where we connect with the cosmos. Similar to how we connect to the physical Earth through our Root chakra, we also connect with the limitless sky of the Universe and the Divine.

It is here where we remember or re-member ourselves and our connection to the Universe and all life. We recognise that we are part of the interconnected web of the cosmos and that we are interconnected with each other, all part of something infinitely bigger than ourselves.

It is through the Crown chakra that we glimpse the bigger picture, access our wisdom and, through this, become aligned with universal energies as we surrender, let go of our need to control outcomes and allow the Universe to work with us, as well as through us; in complete partnership. It is about being fully present, with our presence, in each moment.

We might well find all matter of synchronicities occurring in our lives without us having to do anything. Miracles materialising when we most need them. It is the law of attraction, which is the product of our partnership with the Universe. We might well become aware of the universal energies that are constantly present, including our own presence within our body.

However, overstimulation of this chakra, as well as armouring this chakra, can lead to issues of feeling ungrounded, unable to determine reality, or feel connected with reality. Staying in the moment might prove difficult as we might time travel to the past or future in our minds. Consequently, we never quite land or connect with our environment and others.

Alternatively, armouring can show up as cynicism, lack of joy, faith or trust in life, as well as the process of life itself.

Power Animal Chakra Journey

Now that you have gained some insight into the chakras and how they work within you, you can use the following Power Animal chakra journey to gain further insights into them.

The chakra explanations I have provided are by no means exhaustive, they only touch the surface and are based on my personal experience of them. Ultimately it is only through your own personal journey, exploration and connection with your own energy centres that you can begin to experience them for yourself, thereby developing your own understanding of them.

You can use the Power Animal chakra journey for each chakra by setting your intention for which chakra you need your Power Animal's guidance with. Remember to also visualize the colour of the chakra you need support with.

First make sure that you are not going to be disturbed. This includes switching off your mobile phone.

You can either sit upright in a chair, lay down or sit cross-legged on the floor. It is important that you are in contact with the ground and this reality.

Before you start, set your intention regarding which chakra you would like to explore. You can do this by stating out loud or in your mind, that you are asking for the support of a Power Animal who can act as your guide within this chakra.

Have a glass of water ready for after the journey.

1. Before you close your eyes, take careful note of the room you are in, noticing all there is to notice about it.
2. Once you are ready, close your eyes and take three deep inhalations.
3. As your breath deepens, begin breathing into the chakra you want to work with. Do this by first identifying where it is located in your body. Next visualise its colour. And finally begin to take your breath down into it. If it is your crown or throat, then you need to visualise breathing into it too.

4. As you inhale into the chakra, watch it grow bigger and bigger until it appears as a circular doorway in front of you.

5. When you are ready, step through the doorway into the world beyond.

6. What do you notice about the environment, the atmosphere?

7. As you explore, you notice signs of life, until you see a Power Animal approach you and invite you to follow.

8. Spend some time exploring this environment with your Power Animal guide, taking note of all your Power Animal has to show you, as it will be a message that will help you understand this aspect of yourself.

9. When your Power Animal has finished showing you what you need to see, they will guide you back to the entrance of the chakra.

10. Remember to give thanks for their support, then go back through the chakra doorway.

11. As you inhale, begin to visualise the chakra doorway getting smaller and the room you began your journey in

becoming sharper and more focused.

12. Wiggle your toes and fingers before opening your eyes.

13. Take time to orientate yourself, and when ready, gently sit up and drink the glass of water, taking your time to ground in the present moment.

14. Journal about your experience, noting down any insights or questions that come to you.

Further Exploration

As stated throughout, the contents of this book just touch the surface of how you can work with your Power Animals and the chakras.

It is up to you as to how much further you wish to explore. There has been much written about Power Animals; there are many Shamanic Practitioners and Shamans around the world who work with them in their own ways.

You can explore further by browsing the internet, or finding a course that will best suit you. However, nothing can really compensate for your own experience of working with Power Animals, nor for your own inner-wisdom and understanding.

Wishing you a wonderful adventure,

Naseem Ahsun

Lightning Source UK Ltd.
Milton Keynes UK
UKHW01f2009110518
322484UK00001B/9/P

9 781999 584900